Once Upon A Dream

UK Rhymes

Edited By Sheila Ashwood

First published in Great Britain in 2017 by:

YoungWriters
Est. 1991

Coltsfoot Drive
Peterborough
PE2 9BF
Telephone: 01733 890066
Website: www.youngwriters.co.uk

All Rights Reserved
Book Design by Jenni Harrison
© Copyright Contributors 2016
SB ISBN 978-1-78624-727-8
Printed and bound in the UK by BookPrintingUK
Website: www.bookprintinguk.com
YB0297AZ

FOREWORD

Welcome, Reader!

For Young Writers' latest competition, *Once Upon A Dream*, we gave school children nationwide the task of writing a poem all about dreams, and they rose to the challenge magnificently!

Pupils could write about weird and wonderful dreamlands, aspirations or hopes, or delve into nightmares. They could write about whatever they wanted, the only limits were the limits of imagination! Our aspiring poets have also developed their creative skills along the way, getting to grips with poetic techniques such as rhyme, simile and alliteration to bring their thoughts to life. The result is this entertaining collection that allows us a fascinating glimpse into the minds of the next generation, giving us an insight into their dreams. It also makes a great keepsake for years to come.

Here at Young Writers our aim is to encourage creativity in children and to inspire a love of the written word, so it's great to get such an amazing response, with some absolutely fantastic poems. This made it a tough challenge to pick the winners, so well done to *Sarah Adamson* who has been chosen as the best poet in this anthology.

I'd like to congratulate all the young authors in *Once Upon A Dream - UK Rhymes* - I hope this inspires them to continue with their creative writing.

Sheila Ashwood

CONTENTS

Winner:

Sarah Adamson (10) - Thornley Primary School, Durham — 1

Independent Entries

Katie Adeosun (9) — 3

Buchanhaven School, Peterhead

Gemma Cheyne (9)	4
Jay Robertson (9)	6
Mason Legge (8)	8
Millie Donaldson (9)	9
Joseph Dougal (8)	10
Logan James Ross (9)	11
Isla McRobbie (9)	12
Dominik Grzywacz (9)	13
Adam Thomson (8)	14
Angel Robertson (9)	15
James Green (9)	16
Jacob Hendry (9)	17
Kai Fraser (9)	18
Layla Drunsfield (9)	19
Elissa Sienna Watson (8)	20
Alexa Thom (9)	21
Artjoms Safronenko (9)	22

Gilbert Colvin Primary School, Ilford

Santhipriya Shan (11)	23
Rizwan Haque (10)	24
Rishie Gajendran (10)	25
Saffron Nicole Johnson Spence (10)	26
Aliza Chaudry (10)	27
Khadija Khan (10)	28
Abilaash Rameshbabu (10)	30
Cagena Nyamutumbu (10)	31
Hamid Mohamed Molana (10)	32
Jayda Da Conceicao Albuquerque (10)	33
Rayyan Khan (11)	34
Andria Kyriacou (10)	35
Krish Baranwal (10)	36
Mehek Ghani (10)	37
Haania Hussain Pirani (10)	38
Gursevak Singh (10)	39
Libitha Kamaleswaran (10)	40
Jessica Bennewith (11)	41
Amir Patel (10)	42
Jacob Charlie Parrott (10)	43
Oliver Jaden Barracks (10)	44

Glashieburn Primary School & Nursery, Aberdeen

Deshawn Alenkhe (10)	45
Adanna-Vidya Soronnadi (10)	46
Abigail Chissell (9)	48
Kieran Price (10)	50
Ryan Rattray (10)	51
Emily Ferguson (11)	52
Rose Gill (9)	53
Camille Forth (9)	54
Ellen Murray (9)	55
Owen Song (9)	56
Rianna Wemyss (10)	57
Chloe Mundie (9)	58
Jessica Lawson (10)	59
Fatima Al Zahra (11)	60

Evie-Mae Graciela Scoble (9)	61
Gemma Murdoch (10)	62
Daniel Hems (9)	63
Charlotte Pendrey (9)	64
Sophie Walker (10)	65
Syeda Malahim Fatima (10)	66
Esmé Annand (9)	67
Alexa Chan (10)	68
Abigail McConnachie (10)	69
Erica Margaret Torliefson (10)	70
Neve Christie (9)	71
Scott Fraser (10)	72
Lia Kari (9)	73
Ewan Lamb (8)	74
Connor Murray (9)	75
Imogen Hosie (10)	76
Simon Alexander Scott (9)	77
Aidan Neal (9)	78
Lauren Ella Henderson (9)	79
Josh Combe (9)	80
Dua Fatima (9)	81
Abby Wood (9)	82
Findlay Middleton (9)	83
Ben Masson (10)	84

Kirkhill School, Aberdeen

Lauren Norrie (10)	85
Carly Mcintosh (10)	86
Dylan Ingram (11)	88
Iona Matson (11)	89
Kieran Bailey Matheson (11)	90
Alana Thomson (10)	91
C J Brownlee (10)	92
Connor Mitchell (11)	93
Mackenzie Clarke (10)	94
Megan Mitchell (9)	95
Lauren Milne (11)	96
Harley Clelland (11)	97
Shannon Lever (10)	98
Lana Cartney (10)	99
Aaron Cameron (11)	100
Ella Rose Dunlop (8)	101
Luke Havelock (11)	102

Ewelina Brejza (8)	103
Erin Winters (8)	104
Tegan Gilbride (8)	105
Mya Robb (7)	106
Paige Anderson (9)	107
Weronika Kloska (11)	108
Amie Reid (10)	109
Saul Scott Barclay (9)	110
Ella Rose Cartney (9)	111
Daniel John Craig Taylor (10)	112
Oliver Fraser (8)	113
Aleksandra Wieczorek (7)	114
Jac Stopper (7)	115
Nicholas Lonie (8)	116
Ritchie Milne (8)	117
Lois Anderson (6)	118
Sophie Jane Hawe (6)	119
Kaydyn James Rhind (7)	120
Isla Cheyne (6)	121
Amy Middleton (7)	122
Mya Taylor (6)	123
Nadia Simpson (8)	124
Lennox George Andrew (6)	125
Jason Falconer (8)	126

North Hinksey CE Primary School, Oxford

Hikari Daniels (9)	127
Daniel Armstrong (9)	128
Eva Florence Yoxall-Vale (9)	130
Bella Wilson (9)	132
Verity Broome Saunders (10)	134
Will Hodges (8)	135
Annie Scarborough (10)	136
Lucy Desitter (10)	137
Nicolas Vargas (7)	138
Pippa Scarborough (7)	139

St John's Primary School, Edinburgh

Danny Lewis (9)	140
Freya Auchincloss (9)	142

Tara Divito (10)	144
Finlay McWilliam (10)	146
Emily McKenzie (10)	147
James Craig (10)	148
Beth Adams (10)	149
Nicholas Carr (10)	150
Sean Brannen (9)	151
Motiya Muzzamil (9)	152
Himmat Singh (10)	153
Grant Daly (10)	154
Cyprian Kreft (10)	155
Imran Zafar (9)	156
George Davie (10)	157
Callie Dooner (10)	158
Alex Roy (10)	159
Lewis Johnston	160

Katie Jeal (9)	183
Charles Edward Coultas (9)	184
Kai Smith (10)	185
Harry Gibbon (10)	186
Tasha Musgrave (10)	187
Ashley Smith (10)	188
Lily-Mae Gascoyne (10)	189
Ellen Hudson (9)	190
Lewis Wade (9)	191

Thornley Primary School, Durham

Jodie Marie Leigh (10)	161
Katie Elves (10)	162
Lilia Grace Mains (10)	163
Millie Nuttall (10)	164
Ben Hall (10)	165
Emma Jane Stokoe (10)	166
Benjamin Jack Hardy (10)	167

Thornton Dale CE Primary School, Pickering

Sam Halliday (11)	168
Kara Peel (10)	170
Anna Todd (9)	171
Evie Atkinson (10)	172
Nathan Bowes (9)	173
Ruby Lunn (10)	174
Andrew Prole (10)	175
Molly Gwilliam (10)	176
Adam Halliday (9)	177
Libby Horsley (10)	178
Leah Rouph (10)	179
Hollie Buckler (10)	180
Emma Hall (10)	181
Sarah Vasey (10)	182

THE POEMS

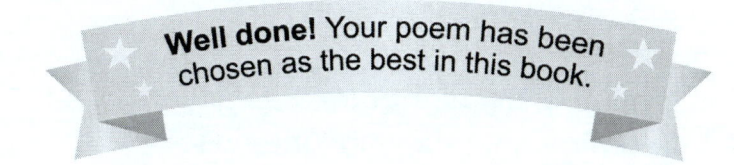

Well done! Your poem has been chosen as the best in this book.

Nightmare To Dream

I close my eyes and drift off to sleep
To a world of dreams that makes me creep
Snakes and tigers, monsters and witches
All fighting for my hidden riches

I battle them hard with my mythical sword
All the time wishing I would be ignored
But more and more I see them coming
Out of the dark I have to start running

I run to a light set into the distance
Hoping for some helpful assistance
I can feel the things getting closer to me
I turn around and drop on one knee

I feel so alone with tears in my eyes
Then my riches inside start to amplify
There's a flash and a bang and the things they vanish
Back to their world, forever banished

I wake from my sleep, knowing I'm free
Safe again under my little oak tree
Oh wait a minute, my nightmare has ended
But I'm dreaming now like I had intended.

Sarah Adamson (10)
Thornley Primary School, Durham

Once Upon A Dream

I wake up in the morning to see my breakfast on my bed,
by the side of it is my teddy called Ted.
I go downstairs and find a brand new table,
the words 'this is for you' written neatly on a label.
I get myself dressed and head off to school,
but everyone laughs and calls me a fool.
I run to a forest and begin to walk through,
I notice the ground is covered in bird poo!
At the end of the forest I see a small light,
I follow it onwards for a whole day and night.
The light suddenly turns and moves toward me,
now I know it's a dream but what could it be?
The light is a fairy who shows me around,
a place where you can sit down on the ground.
The fairy gently takes hold of my hand,
she smiles and says, 'Welcome to Fairyland.'

Katie Adeosun (9)

Space Aliens

Once upon a time I was at school and we were learning about a poem competition.
I started to daydream about what I could write
I thought and I thought and I thought and then an idea came to me.
I was in space, the sky was all purple and blue
I started to float towards an unusual-looking planet.
I got there and at first there was no movement
But after a while I heard a crack.
I started to look around
I saw a green creature staring at me.
I picked it up and started to think.
What is this creature?
Is it an alien? Is it just a balloon?
It can't be a balloon, I thought, *it's moving by itself.*
I decided it must be an alien
So I let it go to see if it would take me to more.
It stood there for a minute then it went away slowly.
I quietly started to follow it away to somewhere unknown.
When we had walked for quite a long while
I started to see a pile of green aliens lying in a hole.
They must have been sleeping, the other one must have woken up before

And it started to go for a walk and then it found me.
After five minutes, the little one poked a bigger one, it could be its mum.
They all started to wake up.
They stopped and stared like the little one did.
All of a sudden they were all around me hugging me
Like a hand in a tight glove.
They stayed there for what felt like an hour.
When I started to walk away they all ran back after me
I stopped and thought, *what a wonderful planet this is!*

Gemma Cheyne (9)
Buchanhaven School, Peterhead

Pokémon Danger

Once upon a time in Palla Town
I woke and watched TV
The news about Pokémon
They said, 'Come to the centre.'
So I got ready, I ran
He said, 'Pick one: Charmander, Squirtle, Bulbasaur'
But he checked, there were none left
So I got Pikachu, he kicked out of his Pokéball
I got a Pokéball and a Pikedex
When you point at it
It will tell you the information
So I left
I saw my first Pokémon
I pointed my Pokédex, it was Charmander
I threw my Pokéball and caught it
It is my favourite Pokémon
I saw my friends Gregor and Adam
Gregor had Squirtle
Adam had Bulbasaur
They had caught one Pokémon as well
Gregor caught Venonat
Adam caught Paras
Then two people came with T-shirts that said
I Stand For Team Massive

It was a boy called Bob
There was a girl called Jessica
They had two Pokémon as well
Jessica had Slowbro
Bob had Sand Slash
I battled them
Before I battled I caught a Squirtle
I chose a Charmander, I won
Charmander evolved to Charmeleon
Then Charmeleon evolved to Charlzard
Then Mega Charlzard.

Jay Robertson (9)
Buchanhaven School, Peterhead

Mars Football League

I was on Mars and it was as orange as fire.
The posts and the crossbar were as white as snow.
I was playing for Ford United.
Our team were against a team that was at the top of the league,
Called FC United.
This game was for the League Cup.
I was star player and team captain, I was also the team's top scorer.
I scored 146 goals in two seasons. FC United got the kick-off.
My brother was in goal.
It was half-time, 0-0.
It was full time and it was still 0-0.
After extra time it was still 0-0.
It went to penalties.
It was 4-4, I was taking the last penalty.
I scored it, 5-4 to Ford United.
We won the League Cup.

Mason Legge (8)
Buchanhaven School, Peterhead

Candyland

One day me and my friend were in Candyland
It was beautiful and we realised it was a dream
We went for a walk to get to our house
We found a gingerbread man walking along the path
Looking as jolly as Santa
When we got to our house we realised we had a pool
We discovered in our house there was a secret room
In it was a bed and a cabinet with a light
We thought it was a master bedroom
But in the master bedroom there was another door
Which led to a massive balcony
That had a table and chairs
Then we went in the pool before bed
We woke up and the dream was all over.

Millie Donaldson (9)
Buchanhaven School, Peterhead

The Sea Trip

I'm loving this hake... I need to go out of my cave and get some more hake.
Haaake! Where are you? I promise I won't hurt you.
I'll just eat you!
I'm pretty far away from home but I just need one piece of hake.
There's one, I'll need to swim fast.
Thirty minutes later. Wait! That's not a hake - that's a *shark!*
Argh! Must find my way back to the cave.
I don't know where I am.
That was a shark, I must be in warmer waters.
I'm so scared, oh my house is right there
I must have swum around the whole world
Oh no! I forgot to get my hake.

Joseph Dougal (8)
Buchanhaven School, Peterhead

Dream Land Funnies

D ream big
R un away in dreams
E verything flying
A smart invention
M illions of things around you

L and far away
A nd creepy things
N o people except friends
D id you go?

F unny stuff happening
U nusual stuff can happen
N othing not cool
N othing not smart
I n the
E nd
S hall you return?

Logan James Ross (9)
Buchanhaven School, Peterhead

BFG

He helps you with your dreams
He makes them come true
He is real
He might be real, nobody knows
He is the Big Friendly Giant
You would like to meet him
And he would like to meet you too
He is not scary, he is so sweet
That's why you would like to meet him.
He wouldn't harm you or your pets 'cause he is harmless.
He would just tell you to climb on his hand
And he would take you on a ride
What is he? The BFG.

Isla McRobbie (9)
Buchanhaven School, Peterhead

Animal Land

I'm in an open land of animals, seeing lots of rabbits, they hop around.
I see a house, I go inside, the walls are like a cat.
Even that cat and dog are following me
I wish they were not there
I don't know what that dog is to me
A friend of a cat and me,
It never seems to be dangerous in the Land of Animals 'cause they're nice and fluffy.
So it's good to be happy in the Land of Animals.

Dominik Grzywacz (9)
Buchanhaven School, Peterhead

Cool Land

One lovely morning I was walking down the path
And the sun had his snazzy glasses on.
I thought they were fantastic
I went to the river
I saw the two buddy penguins hanging out, surfing
I finally arrived at my castle
I decided to go get my swim shorts on and play with the penguins
I felt so energised and happy when I was playing with the penguins
I got my phone and text teleported home.

Adam Thomson (8)
Buchanhaven School, Peterhead

The Candy Kingdom

In the distance a candy kingdom
The beautiful sun sparkling
Me and my family excited
A toffee door and chocolate windows
We were happy and scared
A chocolate fountain, *drip, drip* it goes
We opened the caramel door
Strawberry laces for red carpets
There were marshmallows for guards
Everywhere you go, candy
We need to go
Bye Candy Kingdom.

Angel Robertson (9)
Buchanhaven School, Peterhead

The Candy House

Hi I am James, I let people in my house to have fun.
There are slides made of chocolate bars
The walls are made of candyfloss, you can eat whatever you want.
There once came three boys called Zac, Carter and Joseph
They all liked sport and food so they were happy.
I like all children.
All they did was go down the slide and eat,
But then they went home.

James Green (9)
Buchanhaven School, Peterhead

Siam Park Wonderland

S ongs are being sung by birds
I slands are floating water slides in Siam Park
A tlantic Ocean fish dancing
M ansion with sweeties all over it

P arks everywhere
A pples with melted toffee all over them
R ockers in Siam Park
K eeping candy all over the place.

Jacob Hendry (9)
Buchanhaven School, Peterhead

Candy Land

Last night I was dreaming about Candy Land,
everything was made out of candy!
The flowers were lollipops,
the glass was made out of green laces,
the clouds were candyfloss.
So I looked at the river and it was jelly!
Everything was made out of candy,
it was an amazing dream
and I dreamed of Candy Land every day!

Kai Fraser (9)
Buchanhaven School, Peterhead

Sweet House

In the sweet house it is very yummy because the bricks are made
of gummy bears.
The turrets are made of fairy cakes.
I love the windows, made from waffles, they are yummy.
The bed is made of cake
It is a midnight snack, it is so good.
I love the sofa, made of strawberry cakes.
Me and Evie will eat forever. Yummy!

Layla Drunsfield (9)
Buchanhaven School, Peterhead

Mars Sweetie Land Extraordinaire

Sweetie Land entrance. I went on a rocket flying in the air
Me and Angel found Mars Sweetie Land
We went on it and everything was made out of sweeties
Me and Angel found a mansion
It was made out of sweeties
But then a big marshmallow guy came
So we went into the rocket and flew away.

Elissa Sienna Watson (8)
Buchanhaven School, Peterhead

One Day I...

Was going to see if I could qualify for the Olympics
So I was getting ready
Loads of people were going there
I got there
I was just about to go on the beam
I was so happy
I was delighted
I was going on my last piece - floor
My favourite piece!

Alexa Thom (9)
Buchanhaven School, Peterhead

Caramel Land

C aramel Land
A mazing smells
R eally cool
A dventure
M yself
E xcited
L ooks delicious

L ovely
A mazing
N ice
D ream.

Artjoms Safronenko (9)
Buchanhaven School, Peterhead

My Imaginary Best Friend

The bright sun smiling down on me
And the luscious, green grass crawling on my toes
While I sit on my best friend, his orange fluffy fur against my chest
I know I have no fear for the day ahead of me
I'm as happy as can be with my best friend beside me!

His rainbow-coloured feathers falling off as we soar through the sky
With cotton ball clouds going against us when we fly
I'm as happy as can be with my best friend beside me!

I feel as happy as a baby bird that can finally fly
Like a mouse who has just found a big piece of yellow cheese
Like a hungry, aggressive tiger devouring its prey
I'm as happy as can be with my best friend beside me!

He's my beloved, loving bird with his pointy beak pecking at my arm
With his big blue eyes staring down at me
While he runs through the field his squishy pink tail waggles while he runs
And his long dandelion-looking hair flows in the wind
I'm as happy as can be with my best friend beside me!

Santhipriya Shan (11)
Gilbert Colvin Primary School, Ilford

Aliens And All Of That Rubbish

In the skies little light, little spheres
I wonder what they will all hear?

The aliens have come from the sky
Hope we all can join their flight
They waddled towards us and made a smile
Greeting us, I wished was in style

We gave them food to continue their journey
As for their gratitude they gave us an alien dog
But they demonstrated that it only eats logs

Day after day the dog ate the trees
The council had to pay many more fees
He got so frustrated at what he eats
After that we gave him a chocolate treat

After that day the town was quiet
Oh phew! I thought it would go riot

A UFO came to us, *Oh how will we look after another?*
The dog ran to the UFO looking like he'd hover

The door opened, the aliens came back
An alien showed what all of us lacked
It pulled a gun out, we were dead
I woke up in the comfort of my bed.

Rizwan Haque (10)
Gilbert Colvin Primary School, Ilford

Nightmares Of Clowns

N o one has ever warned me
I n the scary nights
G hosts creep up on me
H owever I try and fight
T aunt is what I do to them
M errily they think I am apparently being pranked
A lways and never this happens to me
R eappearing five times a week
E very time I try to be meek
S ometimes it just can't be

O ccasionally I dreamt of clowns
F earful of their frowns

C reepy are their tricks
L ooking at people like bricks
O ffence is what they do to me
W hen they fly it just can't be
N ever have I wanted to ever meet a clown
S cary is what I think when they make a frown.

Rishie Gajendran (10)
Gilbert Colvin Primary School, Ilford

Nine Cats

I have nine cats
they are as cute as can be
they are better than yours
at least one, two and three

One is as big as a house
two is as small as a mouse
three is mean and green
four does not even have any gravity

Five is as blue as a shoe
six can barely even breathe
seven will never go to Heaven and
eight eats from a bathtub
nine, don't even talk about nine because it's me!

I love my cats especially
one, two and three
so next time you see me
I will be owning 43
I wake up in the morning
realising it's a dream
I turn around and open my eyes
and there are nine cats staring at me!

Saffron Nicole Johnson Spence (10)
Gilbert Colvin Primary School, Ilford

The Drowning Aeroplane

Trying to survive in this busy crowded place
Worse than old grannies having a race
Am I feeling this harsh rain?
Or being an animal, getting tamed?

Uneducated driver
Trying to go higher
I didn't expect this bore
I wanted more

Aeroplane loses direction and fuel
And these crazy people trying to be cool
We fall right down like an egg falling out of its nest
And a tiger finding its prey and being the best

We land and... *boom* we all are doomed
We drown until we reach the bottom
I'm all alone in this isolated ocean that's forgotten!

Aliza Chaudry (10)
Gilbert Colvin Primary School, Ilford

Horrible Haunted House

There was no door
Cobwebs filling its place
I'm too frightened to explore
Let's go!

What?
Mummy, Daddy
Where are you?
They probably went in
Argh!
Get it off
There is a spider on my skin

Luckily I spot a half-open window
I push with all my might
Didn't know it was that tight

It was all dark
I wish I'd gone to the park
What's that sound?
I peep around
Nothing was shown

It's like the world had been finished
But I was too bad to go to Heaven
I'm just eleven

(well nearly)
Hang on what's that...
Khadija Khan (10)
Gilbert Colvin Primary School, Ilford

Dangerous Dinosaurs

Wow! I found a portable teleport
Thinking, *where will it take me?*
Stepping in with a *whoosh!*
But you wouldn't believe where it took me

Flying out like a bird
I landed on Dino Land
There seemed to be lots of roaring
While the trees were soaring

Soon just then a dino showed up
I didn't know if it was a spinosaurus
Or a tyrannosaurus or even a ceratosaurus
But that dino looked hungry!

Just then it gave a shout
And charged at a million miles
But now I'm in trouble, in a big dino rubble.

Abilaash Rameshbabu (10)
Gilbert Colvin Primary School, Ilford

Boys

Grumpy, annoying people I don't like
You should know they're horrible in sight,
Even my dream resists the thought
But is it a nightmare that's had me caught?

Even my brother is my enemy
Well, maybe once my frenemy,
All the nasty boys I wished to have fought
But is it a nightmare that's had me caught?

Boys, boys such a bore
So much more tedious than a long tour,
It is them I should sort
But is it a nightmare that's had me caught?

Luckily it's all a dream
But still boys are what they seem!

Cagena Nyamutumbu (10)
Gilbert Colvin Primary School, Ilford

My Spooky Dream

I can't believe my eyes when I look up to see
A whole new world in front of me
I take a step forward as anxious as can be
Glancing left, right, back and in front of me
But I don't get any luck
All I see is smoke
So I ask myself how did I get here?
I hope this is a joke
Whoosh! Something is lurking around
I really wish I didn't but I see a scary clown
A maniac grin spreads across its pale ghastly face
I run like a lightning bolt but it starts to chase
I trip over and fall in a black hole
And as quick as a flash I am back in bed.

Hamid Mohamed Molana (10)
Gilbert Colvin Primary School, Ilford

Candy Land

How did I get here? I hope this is a joke
I can't believe my eyes
I can see a whole dreamland right in front of me
I feel so lucky, excited and joyful
As my dream has finally come true
I run around in joy as I say, 'I love candy, I love candy'
This is the best day of my life
I taste a bit of the candy cane
My eyes start to glow
I start to think that I am going to live here forever
There're lots of things to do that are cool there
Like chocolate waterfalls, candyfloss trees, gummy bears, raindrops
And much, much more.

Jayda Da Conceicao Albuquerque (10)
Gilbert Colvin Primary School, Ilford

Superhero

S ometimes I wonder where the superheroes go
U p in the sky and away they glow
P reciously waiting for the bad guy to show
E veryone screaming and shouting at the way he says no!
R ampaging through the city on his big, scary machine
H eroes try but plummet to their death
E veryone groans as they're still not saved
R avens squawk as they desperately need help
O n second thoughts the bad guy decides to save the world.

Rayyan Khan (11)
Gilbert Colvin Primary School, Ilford

Miracles

M agic just randomly came to my mind
I suddenly woke up and saw nothing but stars
R unning and running to find a way home
A bunch of magic stars, just swirled around me
C oming to me was also white dust
L ooping and swirling just like a good dancer
E ven though I didn't believe in magic I started to fly up higher and higher
S o much fun flying, then I woke up, it was just a dream, my dream come true.

Andria Kyriacou (10)
Gilbert Colvin Primary School, Ilford

Hello Mr Alicorn!

A n alicorn is a mysterious creature with wings and has a
L ong horn, with a bright pink mane
I t has a rainbow coloured tail, it is so shiny it
C an be seen from miles away. They are
O n point with their colours by far. Their hooves have
R azor-sharp nails. They are not hostile, they will do
N o harm. But as it gets hurt it will go mental and will turn into a
S cary beast.

Krish Baranwal (10)
Gilbert Colvin Primary School, Ilford

A Midsummer Night

It is a midsummer night when I cry my eyes out
And all I can see is fog
I hope it's a lie, my worst fear is realised
I'm stuck with a spider!
A manic grin appears from behind
As I try to run as fast as a flash
And there it is, laughing at me
My heart beats as fast as Usain Bolt
I run and run with my face so red
I close my eyes for some hope
As I awake to see I'm in my lovely safe bed.

Mehek Ghani (10)
Gilbert Colvin Primary School, Ilford

Homework

H omework is not a solution
O ver-exaggerated homework of doom
M ums shout until they go boom!
E ven my dreams do not like my thoughts
W hy is homework even a nightmare?
O ver-thinking about why does it exist?
R eciting songs as the homework distracts
K icking myself when I don't get the question.

Haania Hussain Pirani (10)
Gilbert Colvin Primary School, Ilford

Flying High

I fly so high
In the night sky
I love to soar
Above the rich and poor

I love to lay
Up above the beautiful bay
I love to stare
At people who are taming a bear
Stroking a hare
Or even people with funny fear

Sometimes I like to glide
On some rainbow slides
Oh so high
In the night sky.

Gursevak Singh (10)
Gilbert Colvin Primary School, Ilford

My Wizard Dream

W illing to be a wizard
I feel like I am in a swirling blizzard
Z ipping, zapping with my pet otter
A life like this is just like Harry Potter
R aising my wand like a witch
D oing different spells, feeling like I am rich
R uling the world like the Queen
Y ielding to my dream.

Libitha Kamaleswaran (10)
Gilbert Colvin Primary School, Ilford

Criminal Clowns

C apturing all our funniest memories
L eaving all the worst behind
O n the run from this terrible moment
W ishing, wishing for a miracle
N othing but tears, nothing but sorrow, no happiness is to be shown
S weating and panting under the covers, only realising it's just a nightmare.

Jessica Bennewith (11)
Gilbert Colvin Primary School, Ilford

A New World

I rip and I slash,
I curse and I grow.
I fight and I dash,
Until I drop onto the concrete floor.
My dream is only to free the poor.

I raise my sword and slam it down,
Creating sparks in the gloomy town.
I soar above the starry sky,
In need to stop that high-pitched cry.

Amir Patel (10)
Gilbert Colvin Primary School, Ilford

Opposite Dreams

Up in epic space
Down in the deep blue sea
Completely weird
Seems to be normal
Crazy new worlds
Boring old worlds
Monsters as scary as all the monsters in the world
Beasts that are cute cats
Do you have dreams like this?
Or is it just me?

Jacob Charlie Parrott (10)
Gilbert Colvin Primary School, Ilford

The Football Champion

Goal!
Arsenal won the game
Thanks to me
Oliver Barracks
The world champion
footballer

Kicking the ball
Winning the game
Just because of me
What would Arsenal
Do without me?

Oliver Jaden Barracks (10)
Gilbert Colvin Primary School, Ilford

Pranksters World!

Pranksters World! A pranking place
Even the sun pranks, it's no mistake
The stars come out at twelve noon
And the sun arrives at the time of the moon

It's a miniature world of fear and dread
If you go there on holiday you're surely dead
Even children prank when filled with glee
They prank till they go in for tea

They learn at school how to prank all about
And prank all day without tiring out
If they are pranked they're filled with despair
But when they prank others they don't really care

Because they pranked all day and night
They gave each other scary frights
So now they're dead, down in the grave
And now we can all shout hooray!

Deshawn Alenkhe (10)
Glashieburn Primary School & Nursery, Aberdeen

Once Upon A Dream

As I went to bed that night
I thought of the Queen
And right before my eyes
I was whisked away to be seen
By the Austrian Queen
Her hair, ash-blonde
Her eyes pale blue
And a heart of joy
For me and you

Nothing will make me forget that moment
As I met the Queen of Austria
Her hair wobbled like a vanilla panna cotta
Her voice was soft and silvery
She wore the finest dress made out of lace
How she walked into the room with impossible grace

As I stared behind me and all around
All I could see were robes lined with gold
And servants bringing in our food without a sound
When I looked up I was blinded by the ceiling's beauty
There were paintings of flowers and real chandeliers
I couldn't believe it, I was amazed

Suddenly she began to talk
She said that I could stay there for five years
I couldn't believe this
I had to stay
Right now I am so happy it's unreal
I am staying for five years

As the years went on
I got taught how to eat, talk and drink
Here in Austria.

Adanna-Vidya Soronnadi (10)
Glashieburn Primary School & Nursery, Aberdeen

Once Upon A Dream

My dream has pink fluffy unicorns
Dancing on candy clouds

I relax in my beautiful candy house
Which has marshmallow windows
And a caramel fire
And a chocolate chimney
With a candy cane arch

As the snow flew over my candy house
It made the sound *whoosh!*
I went into the marshmallow elevator
It whizzed me up into the clouds
Where there were trampolines

I felt really cheerful
When I was up there
But I fell and suddenly felt a soft landing
It was a candy snowman
So that was the last of going up there

I met the candy snowman
Who I met when I fell
She said, 'Hello' in a nice voice
She was my friend forever and ever
That is what my dream was about!

A new dream was about to start...
Once upon a dream.

Abigail Chissell (9)
Glashieburn Primary School & Nursery, Aberdeen

Once Upon A Dream

Once upon a time lived
A boy called Jack
He had an imaginative dream
His dream was...
Him in Candy Land
He saw a candy unicorn
He went up to it
He met a Candyfloss Man
He heard a banging noise
Jack went to check it out
And his hands felt like candyfloss
It was amazing and he thought about a house
Jack got it, it had a candy cane arch
And a chocolate door and candyfloss for the windows
The Candyfloss Man said, 'I built it for you'
Jack said, 'Thank you, let's go for a walk'
'Good idea,' said the Candyfloss Man
Jack felt happy here
In the morning Jack was shocked
And leaned forward in his bed...

Kieran Price (10)
Glashieburn Primary School & Nursery, Aberdeen

This Is Me

I'm in a Victorian factory,
With aching ankles and broken bones
And with blizzard blisters and lumpy hands
I'm lucky to get it done by eight
Blood dripping down my sweaty body
I feel I'm dying inside my dehydrated chest
It's like I'm a robot
Shutting down, out of fuel, running out
I say to him, 'Wake up my dearest friend.'
I shall pray to my Lord to help him before he dies
Before he hurts more with pain
Rusting machines and fingers in mills
There's been death after death and injury by injury
Everyone's gone
It must be my turn now, love you dearest Mother
The Victorian times
Are to be continued...

Ryan Rattray (10)
Glashieburn Primary School & Nursery, Aberdeen

Once Upon A Dream

I was in a chrome Lamborghini
Eating a bacon and cheese panini
Outside my local shop
(It smelt as good as a pork chop)

Suddenly I saw a rhino chasing after me
It stopped and started dancing and prancing
Then I heard a roar, then a lion started crying
I got such a shock and I ripped my smelly old sock

I saw blackness then I saw a likeness
I then saw a castle made of purple and pink candyfloss
I heard birds chirping, wind blowing
Old women sewing, everybody smiling.

I jump in a pool (with rainbow sequins)
I have a bubbly hot tub
I rest my eyes while I think of my chess club.

Emily Ferguson (11)
Glashieburn Primary School & Nursery, Aberdeen

Once Upon A Dream

In a forest nice and green
There were goblins, short and lean
I'm with a stranger and my friend
And I'll be with them till the end
It was as scary as a zombie game
I want it to end, I can't bear the pain
It was hard to destroy them all
Especially when you're surrounded by trees, nice and tall
You could hear the trees whispering and rustling
And all of the birds chirping and singing
Quietly and quickly I grabbed goblins left and right
Making sure to hold them tight
I hope that we can end this quest soon
Hopefully before the full moon.

Rose Gill (9)
Glashieburn Primary School & Nursery, Aberdeen

Once Upon A Dream

Once I fell asleep
That was very, very deep
I woke up very dizzy, knowing of the strange land
And I understood the land very clearly
Five black figures danced in the sky
They were black Pegasi
That loved walking
As much as talking
I was so excited, happy and enthusiastic
I saw ten small diamonds with legs, arms, head, wings and tails
They are blue with long nails
My dream is a wildlife heaven
It has historic animals, imaginary and real
Then after playing a game with every single animal
I fell asleep again
Then I woke up in the morning.

Camille Forth (9)
Glashieburn Primary School & Nursery, Aberdeen

Candy Land

I was in Candy Land
The candyfloss snow was as fluffy as the clouds

The unicorns' horns were sparkling
Like a thousand jewels in the sunlight

Me and Burger Man saw a mountain made of ice cream
Taller than Mount Everest

We decided to climb it because at the top
There was a giant Cadbury chocolate Flake
Which was as yummy as a chocolate cake

We got there, the chocolate Flake was delicious
We started eating the ice cream as we came down
And we went home afterwards.

Ellen Murray (9)
Glashieburn Primary School & Nursery, Aberdeen

The Museum

T he museum is a special place
H ats were popular in history
E very museum has some famous people in them

M useums are because they carry artefacts from decades past
U nder a museum could be buried artefacts
S ome people were smart and invented things, some just wanted to be regular
E very scientist invents a machine or a saying
U se your brain and maybe you can invent something like the Victorians
M any people invented things like the telephone.

Owen Song (9)
Glashieburn Primary School & Nursery, Aberdeen

Once Upon A Dream

I'm in a universe deep into space
And I'm going to save my poodle
With the help of Clio
The guards are tigers
They're as fierce as fire
I ran as fast as light
But the tigers followed

The walls were solid
Clio the alien was as sneaky as a lion hunting
I found my poodle and me and my poodle and Clio
Flew away through the clouds
It felt like cotton candy
The tigers turned the world upside down
Now birds peck my feet and the clouds knock me over.

Rianna Wemyss (10)
Glashieburn Primary School & Nursery, Aberdeen

The Butterfly Beauty Salon

Once upon a dream the Butterfly Beauty Salon stood there tall and fair
In and out customers flew and always leaving looking brand new!
Me and my three best friends at the desk
Always trying to smile our best
All the work is so much fun
Like sitting all day in the nice hot sun!
We answer phone calls as politely as possible
And we smile so much we go as pink as a blossom
And after a busy day of very hard work
We get some hot chocolate and have a slurp!

Chloe Mundie (9)
Glashieburn Primary School & Nursery, Aberdeen

Once Upon A Dream

I am in a dream
Just once again
The clouds look like candyfloss
And the river looks like chocolate
The houses look like sweets
And taste like sweets too
But that's not all
The paths are made of bubblegum
And the walls are made of sherbet
The sun is made of fudge and
The sea is filled with cola and lots of candy fish
This will be the very last thing
The castles are made with jelly and
The sand is made of sugar.

Jessica Lawson (10)
Glashieburn Primary School & Nursery, Aberdeen

Once Upon A Dream...

Once upon a dream I was in a magical Candyland
Elves, fairies, goblins, witches and castles, it was mayhem
With a chocolate castle as striking as a diamond
The sun dancing with joy
And a little boy
When I came across my house it was unbelievable
Chocolate walls with an ice cream roof and a hard toffee door
With wafer windows and a Coke pond
Suddenly it started to snow but it wasn't cold
But now it's time to sleep on our lolly bed.

Fatima Al Zahra (11)
Glashieburn Primary School & Nursery, Aberdeen

Once Upon A Dream...

I love dance
Dance is so much fun!
I love dance
I want to be number one!
As I grow up I get better every day
All I hear from the crowd is hip hip hooray!
I love dance
I can pirouette and arabesque
I love dance
I want to be the best!
I can do leaps and glissades
Rond de jambes and sautes
But when I first got into splits I was in quite a daze!
I love dance
Dance is my life
I love dance
Dance is my future.

Evie-Mae Graciela Scoble (9)
Glashieburn Primary School & Nursery, Aberdeen

The Unicorn!

There I was just standing there
Watching a rainbow fly high
In Unicorn Land!

There she was passing by
Flying in circles through the baby-blue sky
In Unicorn Land!

I hopped on her fluffy back
She ran into a cloud with a big smack
In Unicorn Land!

Her rainbow mane neatly braided
But then sadly the image faded
Of Unicorn Land

I wish I could go back
To Unicorn Land.

Gemma Murdoch (10)
Glashieburn Primary School & Nursery, Aberdeen

Once Upon A Dream

Once upon a dream...
I woke up in a big, big desert
I saw my best friend Ryan
Why was he here? I thought
Why was I here?
How did I get here? I thought
Ryan pressed a button
The ground started to shake
Then the sand turned into sugar
It started to rain soda
A big jelly castle and jelly houses
With chocolate bar beds
I was very tired
Then I woke up back in my bed.

Daniel Hems (9)
Glashieburn Primary School & Nursery, Aberdeen

Once Upon A Dream

So there I was
Sailing away from Aberdeen
With my friend Imogen
We were sailing to travel the amazing world right in front of us
We felt so adventurous because this was big for us
We hadn't done anything like this before!
Then halfway through the trip we got stuck in Australia
We were so scared
Then we had to live there
It was like we invaded their land
It was so bad we fled to another.

Charlotte Pendrey (9)
Glashieburn Primary School & Nursery, Aberdeen

The Crazy Unipegs

Unipegs, unipegs are the best
They dance on rainbows with no rest

When it snows it just whooshes past
And when it rains it drifts very fast

Unicorn days go as fast as a cheetah
Because they play and laugh and say

You are as happy as can be
You can sing songs and so can we

Goodbye, farewell to you
But remember you're just like us too.

Sophie Walker (10)
Glashieburn Primary School & Nursery, Aberdeen

Once Upon A Dream

Me and my friends were at the movies eating popcorn
The movie was about a unicorn
Suddenly the unicorn popped out
One leg at a time, everyone began to shout
I stared, she was beautiful
Someone called Newsround
I went to her and took her out of the cinema
My friend Ellen had a stable
I was going to take her there
She asked me, 'Where are we going?'
She talked...!

Syeda Malahim Fatima (10)
Glashieburn Primary School & Nursery, Aberdeen

Zombie Nightmare...

Is he here...?
Not too far away!
You'd better be careful
He is here!

He lurks around for human brains
You catch his sight... you're doomed!
I would just run for my life
If I was you!

The zombie babysitter
Is slouching in his living room
He is tall and torn
And as deadly as could be

My world, just stay away.

Esmé Annand (9)
Glashieburn Primary School & Nursery, Aberdeen

Once Upon A Dream

I love gymnastics
It's my whole, entire world!

I love gymnastics
My favourite part is vault
i work really hard so I can be number one!

I train nearly every single day
When I'm at a competition I always hear a yay!

I love gymnastics
I want to be in the Olympics
That's my biggest dream!

Alexa Chan (10)
Glashieburn Primary School & Nursery, Aberdeen

Once Upon A Dream...

All around me I can see rainbows, butterflies, unicorns and candy
My version of Dream Land with lots of fun, plenty of laughter
After a while we all had a snack, can you guess?
Candyfloss, gobstoppers, brainlickers and lots more sweets
After our snack we all went to ride on our unicorns, our own unicorns, till tea
Then off to bed, which by the way, was a cloud.

Abigail McConnachie (10)
Glashieburn Primary School & Nursery, Aberdeen

To Be A Teacher

T o live my dream
O pen up my life

B e amazing
E ngaging lessons

A lways be kind

T o love my class
E nd my childhood
A ct out my life
C are about people
H elp others
E xcellent reports
R espect the world.

Erica Margaret Torliefson (10)
Glashieburn Primary School & Nursery, Aberdeen

American Candies

A mazing American candies
M any different flavours
E ating American candies, both so sour and sweet
R ainbow candies are so cool and squishy
I magine all the flavours and colours you still have to discover
C ake your senses with many flavours and colours to enjoy
A mazing American candies.

Neve Christie (9)
Glashieburn Primary School & Nursery, Aberdeen

Outside Playtime

P laying was the time of my life
L ast place we were in our house
A t the time, in the house, I was on my iPad
Y ay I'm out to play!
T he birds are chirping
I n the trees
M ost of the time the leaves are shaken
E nd of the day we go back home.

Scott Fraser (10)
Glashieburn Primary School & Nursery, Aberdeen

Spiders

S piders are scary
P lus they are hairy
I n some countries spiders are *huge!*
D isastrous spiders, so you will find
E very country has its own kind
R ain is a spider's enemy but I don't mind
S ome spiders are small, so you can't see them at all!

Lia Kari (9)
Glashieburn Primary School & Nursery, Aberdeen

At A Football Match

F ootball is fun
O ne day I'll go to Spain and play Barcelona
O nce I score I celebrate
T errific players and terrifying players
B est football is when you score
A mazed when you score more
L ike people cheering
L ook he scored an amazing goal!

Ewan Lamb (8)
Glashieburn Primary School & Nursery, Aberdeen

Once Upon A Dream

Unicorns, unicorns are the best
They dance on the moon with the rest

When it snows it just *whooshes* past
But when it rains it's like a stone hitting my head

The sun comes out to play all day
And the moon comes out to play all night and they are always playing.

Connor Murray (9)
Glashieburn Primary School & Nursery, Aberdeen

A Tour Around The World!

W e travelled around the world, I was feeling amazing
O n our tour Bobby Joe and I saw the Empire State Building
R ound and round we went to each country
L eave each country every night but excited to roam!
D id Bobby Joe and I ever find a place to call home?

Imogen Hosie (10)
Glashieburn Primary School & Nursery, Aberdeen

The Statue Of Liberty

L iberty Island is in New York
I dream about seeing Liberty Island
B ig dreams are great
E veryone there is happy
R eally you can go inside the Statue of Liberty
T he Statue of Liberty is huge
Y ou would like it too.

Simon Alexander Scott (9)
Glashieburn Primary School & Nursery, Aberdeen

Untitled

I was on a big island
With all of my family
When I saw a big plane going to Florida
But it was not real, it was a dream
I feel happy because I am still on the island
The sun smiled down on me
I could play Minecraft all day.

Aidan Neal (9)
Glashieburn Primary School & Nursery, Aberdeen

Once Upon A Dream

D ream of love and kindness
R ead lots of books
E njoy everything you do in life
A lot of people like reading
M agical books will shine like the stars
S uper books help you live a smart life.

Lauren Ella Henderson (9)
Glashieburn Primary School & Nursery, Aberdeen

Fighting In The Galaxy!

D ream a dream of fighting the galaxy!
R ead, read my story a long, long time ago
E arth is never safe from now on!
A liens are green, greedy goblins!
M edal belongs to me and my friend Cactus!

Josh Combe (9)
Glashieburn Primary School & Nursery, Aberdeen

The Busy Bees

Once upon a dream there was a salon
That was busy as a bee
In and out customers flew
People glitter like disco balls
Customers filled with joy as they leave
The salon spreads around town like migrating birds.

Dua Fatima (9)
Glashieburn Primary School & Nursery, Aberdeen

Once Upon A Dream

S pace is a nice place
P laying a game with my friends, I won the race
A new planet we discover
C an we fly to a new amazing planet?
E nter a new place in space.

Abby Wood (9)
Glashieburn Primary School & Nursery, Aberdeen

Once Upon A Dream

F un in the forest
O ver and under the trees
R unning around
E xciting to go there
S unlight peeking through
T hrowing autumn leaves in the air!

Findlay Middleton (9)
Glashieburn Primary School & Nursery, Aberdeen

My Pet Hamster

H ilarious ball of fur
A ctually amazing
M onstrous pet
S neaky
T errific and fun
E scape artist
R uns as fast as a flash.

Ben Masson (10)
Glashieburn Primary School & Nursery, Aberdeen

Untitled

Once upon a dream I woke up in Mini Land
In Mini Land there were slithering snakes sneaking through the grass
The tiny clouds were dancing in the sky
Tiny little kids were throwing Frisbees into windows, *crash, bang!*
The trees were as colourful as M&Ms

There was a green, greedy gummy bear man
Moving towards the house
The small dog was singing on top of a mountain like a wolf
The flower pots made a bang when the wind blew them over. *Smash!*
The sky was as bright as a highlighter

Cars were going as fast as jets, they crashed, *bang!*
The small footballs were dashing through the grass
The great, giant humans came over and squashed all of the houses.

Lauren Norrie (10)
Kirkhill School, Aberdeen

Once Upon A Dream In Chocolate Land

The sky was as blue as a sapphire glowing
The clumsy, crazy, creative cloud coloured the sky
The people in Chocolate Land are as tough as old boots
Everything in Chocolate Land is edible

The big, bad, brown, bold bear bounced off the bin and fell onto the little bunnies
The tiny tree waved in the wind
The grass was as sweet as a juicy pineapple
A stone suddenly flew through a window. *Smash!*

The horrible, hated, hairy hare ate the terrified, tiny tortoise
The thunder roared! *Bang!*
The forest was full of Thornton's chocolate advent calendars
Santa Claus comes in summer because he thinks it's as hot as lava

The sun has a cheesy grin on his face
The cloud started to cry
Smack! The stars smacked against each other
The wind screamed all through Chocolate Land.

Carly Mcintosh (10)
Kirkhill School, Aberdeen

Thunder

Thunder as loud as a tiger's roar
Thunder is so loud it can't be ignored
Thunder is so loud it goes *boom! Boom! Boom!*
Thunder is loud!

Thunder is as loud as a fire alarm
Thunder is so loud it causes harm
Thunder is so loud it makes me shake like a leaf
Thunder is loud!

Thunder is as loud as a zip line crashing
Thunder is so loud I hate the bashing
Thunder is so loud it screams and shouts in the midnight sky
Thunder is loud!

Thunder is as loud as a tree falling
Thunder is a cold voice in the air calling
Thunder is so loud I can't sleep
Thunder is so loud it wakes me up from my dream
Thunder is loud!

Dylan Ingram (11)
Kirkhill School, Aberdeen

Untitled

Once upon a dream I was in Candy Land
The ground was bouncy like jelly
Cotton candy clouds clambered in the sky
Walking down a honeycomb road, *crunch, crunch*
I licked a toffee apple off a tree, *munch, munch*

The chocolate river screamed as it tumbled over the waterfall
The houses were as chewy as they could be
The candy people smiled wherever they went
The sun was a fried egg with a runny egg yolk

When it rained it tasted like Coca-Cola
A crunchy cookie avalanche raced down the mountain
The strawberry shoelace snake slithered silently through the grass
I ate my way through it all *munch, munch.*

Iona Matson (11)
Kirkhill School, Aberdeen

Funland

Once upon a dream in Funland
The sky was as blue as a super shiny sapphire
The clouds were white and fluffy like snow
And the sun smiled in the big, bright sky

Rivers ran as fast as Usain Bolt
The grass was shiny like an emerald
The trees were as dark as chocolate
The leaves danced around all day

The people were sweet like sugar
The people were helpful just like elves
The people were small like Smurfs
They were everywhere like an army of ants

The weather was hot like lava
There was super white snow on the ground
The clouds were crying giant tears
And the wind was everywhere like a disease.

Kieran Bailey Matheson (11)
Kirkhill School, Aberdeen

Once Upon A Dream

The colourful, cool, chatty cloud danced through the whining wind
Smash! The tree fell to the ground, the clouds were as fat as a cow

The big, bad, bouncy boomerang went flying into the crying cloud
The boomerang is as fast as a cork coming off a bottle
Kaboom! The boomerang exploded

The hopping, hairy, hyper hedgehog climbed up the tall talking tree
Prickle! The hedgehog fell into the cool, cold water, the water was as cold as an ice cream

The big, brown, bouncy bear swam in the sleeping sea
Splash! He caught a fat fish
The bear was brown like a bar of chocolate.

Alana Thomson (10)
Kirkhill School, Aberdeen

Land Of Food

Once in a dream I was in a land of food
Giant pizzas with toppings as colourful as a rainbow
Tomato ketchup went over the hot dog - *squirt!*
The plates were spinning like a record player
The hot dog got shot and started bleeding tomato ketchup
All the animals were as tasty as a hot dog with tomato ketchup
A burger was jumping up and down, *bang! Bang! Bang!*
The sun was an egg with a bright yellow, runny yolk
The banana was undressing
A cracker got hit by an apple, *crack!*
A slice of bacon was burned like charcoal
The potato was yellow like the sun.

C J Brownlee (10)
Kirkhill School, Aberdeen

In My Dream I Am In A Land Of Clouds

The cheerful, creative clouds chatted in the sky
The clouds are as fluffy as a woolly jumper
The clouds are balls of cotton candy in the sky
The clouds sped away, *whoosh!*

The sand clouds cried all the rain out
Whist the cheerful, cool clouds coloured in the sky
The clouds were as cold as ice
The clouds breathed smoke from a rocket
Cough! Splut!
The clouds screamed in the wind! 'Argh!'
The clever clouds creatively climbed the mountain
The cloud is Plasticine waiting to change shape
The clouds are as plain as a piece of paper.

Connor Mitchell (11)
Kirkhill School, Aberdeen

Once Upon A Dream In Unicorn Candyland...

Bang! The fluffy unicorn clashed into the candy tree
The candy sun was as hot as fire
The candy cane trees were dancing in the wind
The slippery, slimy strawberry lace sneaked away

The gummy bear was as red as Hell
The shiny chocolate bar wrappers were winking at me from above
Bang! The hard toffee door slammed shut
The cotton candy cloud clapped at me

The M&M plants were as colourful as the rainbow
The little chocolate bar kids were as small as Smurfs
The unicorn was as soft as cotton candy
The rainbow was stretched across the sky.

Mackenzie Clarke (10)
Kirkhill School, Aberdeen

Love Land, A Place With Love

I am in a lovely love land and there are love hearts everywhere
And I have lovely people with me like my lovely big brother and my lovely little brother
And my lovely mum and my lovely dad
And my lovely first BFF Jayden and my lovely friend Paige
And I can see lots of lovely chocolate houses and lots of lovely waterfalls
And lots of lovely little puppies, cute as the light sky
And I get lost in a cave and I go left and right to get out
And I finally get out and I feel excited and happy at the same time
And there is a chocolate land close by.

Megan Mitchell (9)
Kirkhill School, Aberdeen

Once In A Dream I Landed In Space

The stars were shiny like crystals
And they shoot like jets across the sky
They winked at me again and again
It's like Heaven

Once in a dream I landed in space
The comets were zooming past, *whoosh!*
Off they went as fast as a motorbike
Colourful, cool comets carrying on in the sky
The comet is dancing around in the sky

Once in a dream perfect pink and purple planets play in the sky
The planet is as rough as sandpaper
Saturn is hula hooping all day long
Watch the planets smash into each other
Boom! Boom! Boom!

Lauren Milne (11)
Kirkhill School, Aberdeen

My Dream Is About Leprechauns, Ice Cream And Fire

A lucky, lively leprechaun leaped onto a leaf
The lake was as green as an emerald
A rainbow shot across the sky! *Whoosh!*
The cloud clapped loudly like applause

Ice cream melts quicker than a snowman
I eat ice cream loudly, *slurp, slurp, slurp*
The chocolate ice cream cone is teasing me to eat it
Ice cream is as cold as the iceberg that sank the Titanic

The fire dances across the moonlight
Fireworks in the sky, *boom, boom, bang*
The firework is colourful like Smarties
The fire's like the hot, steamy sun.

Harley Clelland (11)
Kirkhill School, Aberdeen

Once Upon A Dream Under The Sea

Once upon a dream under the sea
Inky octopi were dancing along the sand
The fish were as colourful as a rainbow
Seaweed danced in the current

Sharks swam towards me with jaws snapping, *snap, snap, snap*
The boat wiggled to the bottom of the sea
Lights shone down on me from the land above like sea lights
The soft sand was yellow as the sun

Marvellous, magical mermaids move throughout the sea
The turtle is as slow as a slug
The coral shone as bright as a diamond
Beautiful, bright, bursting bubbles, *pop, pop, pop!*

Shannon Lever (10)
Kirkhill School, Aberdeen

I Live In A Cloud

I live in a happy cloud
My cloud is as white and as creamy as a McFlurry
Super soft and satisfying to sit on
The sun always smiles at me

I live on a sad cloud
My cloud is sulky, full of sorrow and always sniffling
My cloud is sad like cancer
Tears hit the ground like *drip! Drop! Drip! Drop!*

I live on an angry cloud
My cloud is furiously frustrated and fiery
My cloud is angry like an erupting volcano
Bang! Boom! Bang! Boom!
My cloud throws a tantrum and lightning shoots out.

Lana Cartney (10)
Kirkhill School, Aberdeen

Untitled

Up in the sky I see
The sun hugging the snow
The snow smiling at the clouds
Beautiful bluebirds burping in the sky
Clouds are fluffy cotton balls

The disgusting dirt is sleeping in the dark
The slippery snake slithered into a hole
The river goes *whoosh*
The flowers were as yellow as the sun

A super slippery submarine dozing off
Dark blue fish swimming as fast as lightning
Wise whales sing in a choir
Beautiful bubbles burst, *pop! Pop! Pop!*

Aaron Cameron (11)
Kirkhill School, Aberdeen

The Dream In Heaven

On a dark, clear night there was a little girl called Cally
Her mum was fast asleep and so was her five-year-old brother
On that very same day Cally prayed
She wished she could meet an angel
At 12 o'clock an angel appeared at the bottom of Cally's bed
The angel gave Cally a quest
The angel took Cally to Heaven
Then the angel showed Cally the angel's house
The house was made of candyfloss and clouds and bluebells
Cally helped the angel, after she helped the angel she got a reward.

Ella Rose Dunlop (8)
Kirkhill School, Aberdeen

In My Dream I Went To Crazy Land

In my dream I went to Crazy Land
The little lion likes lollipops
The sun peeked behind a cloud
The clouds clapped happily
The snakes slithered slowly

The planet exploded - *bang!*
The sun is as hot as hot lava
The clouds were dancing across the sky
The clouds are like cotton candy

The sharks crashed into rocks, *bing, bang, boom!*
The experiment went *bang!*
The cars crashed - *boom!*
The clouds sped away - *whoosh!*

Luke Havelock (11)
Kirkhill School, Aberdeen

My Ghost Nightmare

On a cold, cold night
I saw a smoky figure
It said, 'Hi!' in a scary voice
I didn't know what it was
It was a ghost, it was doing gymnastics
It had red eyes
It had a beautiful dress on
It pushed all the books off my bookshelf
It went *crash! Bang!*
At the end it ate one hundred pizzas
It seemed like a good ghost but it wasn't
It scared me, it scared my dog
I was with nobody at my house
I got extremely scared.

Ewelina Brejza (8)
Kirkhill School, Aberdeen

Dream

D reaming is a wondering adventure
R ed roses blooming everywhere in my dreams
E very day I see my friend, Ghost
A friendly ghost does not scare me
M y Dreamland is hot as the sun can be
L ovely things everywhere
A once upon a dream poem
N ever-ending adventure
D id you know friendly ghosts live there?

Erin Winters (8)
Kirkhill School, Aberdeen

Unicorn Sensation

D reaming and going to Unicorn Land
R ainbows every single day
E very day unicorns dancing
A candy house in the middle of Unicorn Land
M y friends, Dylan, Logan and Erin helping on journeys
L ovely things everywhere you go
A nd beautiful roses blooming
N ever-ending adventure
D own in Dream Land.

Tegan Gilbride (8)
Kirkhill School, Aberdeen

Untitled

I go to bed with Missy my dog
I dream about a land that is covered in fog
It is Candy Land!
Candy Land is full of candy
Candy and sweets
There are biscuit houses and caramel streets
The waterfalls are chocolate
Me and Missy's favourite were the chocolate waterfalls
Lucy and Lily were there
Missy barked as loud as a bear.

Mya Robb (7)
Kirkhill School, Aberdeen

Untitled

My imaginary house has a chocolate fountain in the house and marshmallows
I feel a little bit sad but really happy
There are lots of people
Their names are Jamie-Lee, Ella C, Jayden, Dylan, Liam and Tony C
You can get anything you want
The place is called Dream Land
And I can see everything
And I can see my imaginary house.

Paige Anderson (9)
Kirkhill School, Aberdeen

Dream

The crazy clouds were playing hide-and-seek with the sun
The clouds were as small as a mouse
The clouds were quickly drifting down and, *bang, smash*
The creative clouds were drawing a picture
The cool clouds were chatting
The clouds were playing with the wool
The curious clouds were watching down below curiously.

Weronika Kloska (11)
Kirkhill School, Aberdeen

Unicorn Land

Me and my BFF are in her house
We go outside to play and we find a plane
We got a scare then we went in the plane
It had pink and blue seats
We flew to the moon
And we got to eat our lunch on the moon
And unicorns invaded the moon
We flew home on a unicorn.

Amie Reid (10)
Kirkhill School, Aberdeen

Once Upon A Dream

The hotels are made out of chocolate bars
The beds are made out of spaghetti
The sofas are made out of bread
The shower is made out of a cup
And hot chocolate comes out of the shower head
The tap is made out of marshmallows
And the TV is made out of chicken nuggets.

Saul Scott Barclay (9)
Kirkhill School, Aberdeen

Magic Land

I am in Magic Land where all your wishes come true
I am with my dad, mum and my sister Lana
I can see a white, creamy cloud
A magic wizard appeared and said,
'I will grant all your wishes
You need to get ingredients.'
I feel happy, excited and amazed.

Ella Rose Cartney (9)
Kirkhill School, Aberdeen

Adventure In Techland

In the year 2020 at 6.49 in the morning
I went to what seemed like the kitchen
and had some coffee to start my day
I ran outside and saw the greenest grass in the world
And just then, surprise! A monkey jumped on my head.

Daniel John Craig Taylor (10)
Kirkhill School, Aberdeen

The Nice Dream

Last night in my big bed
I had a nice dream
I dreamt all about fruits and vegetables
I was in the middle of the fruit and vegetables
I ate the fruits and vegetables
And I felt like a cat that was starving.

Oliver Fraser (8)
Kirkhill School, Aberdeen

Monster Dream

Last night in my sweet bed
I had a scary dream
I dreamed all about a dog, cat, rabbit, horse and monster
The dog and cat were cute, the rabbit was fluffy
The horse was sweet but the monster was ugly.

Aleksandra Wieczorek (7)
Kirkhill School, Aberdeen

Dreamy

D amp as a rainforest
R ed as little ants
E lves are like little red ants
A n animatronic called Freddy
M y hair is floating
Y our hair is not floating.

Jac Stopper (7)
Kirkhill School, Aberdeen

Untitled

Last night in my amazing bed
I had a weird dream
All about running in and out of a mirror
It had a ghost head
It looked mysterious and it was shiny
And it made me feel different.

Nicholas Lonie (8)
Kirkhill School, Aberdeen

Ritchie's Dream

Last night in my big bed
I had a wonderful dream
All about a zombie
The zombie was green
The zombie had no head
The zombie had no feet
I felt scared.

Ritchie Milne (8)
Kirkhill School, Aberdeen

Untitled

Last night in my sweet bed
I had a scary dream
I dreamt all about someone following me
She had sharp nails
She had sharp teeth
It made me feel frightened.

Lois Anderson (6)
Kirkhill School, Aberdeen

Fluffy Unicorn

Last night in my amazing bed
I had an exciting dream
I dreamt about a fluffy unicorn
It was fluffy and cute and sparkly
It made me feel excited and happy.

Sophie Jane Hawe (6)
Kirkhill School, Aberdeen

Untitled

Last night in my waterbed
I had a shocking dream
I dreamt about a mini rocker
It could do stunts and wheelies and backflips
It made me feel brilliant.

Kaydyn James Rhind (7)
Kirkhill School, Aberdeen

Operation

Last night in my glimmering bed
I had a fantastic dream
I dreamt all about operating on somebody
It felt so funny, yucky
And it looked so disgusting.

Isla Cheyne (6)
Kirkhill School, Aberdeen

Sweetie House

Last night in my small bed
I had an exciting dream
I dreamt all about a sweetie house
Sweet, delicious and scrumptious
It made me feel excellent.

Amy Middleton (7)
Kirkhill School, Aberdeen

Untitled

Last night in my comfy bed
I had an exciting dream
I dreamt all about a rabbit
Fluffy, cute and happy
It made me feel great.

Mya Taylor (6)
Kirkhill School, Aberdeen

Untitled

Last night in my beautiful bed
I had a happy dream
I dreamt about pancakes
Delicious, fine and tasty
It made me happy.

Nadia Simpson (8)
Kirkhill School, Aberdeen

Untitled

Last night in my bed
I had a warm dream
I dreamt all about a triceratops
Horned, scary, massive
It made me feel happy.

Lennox George Andrew (6)
Kirkhill School, Aberdeen

Untitled

Last night in my comfy bed
I had a happy dream
I dreamt about a rabbit
Cute, cuddly and fluffy
It made me feel happy.

Jason Falconer (8)
Kirkhill School, Aberdeen

My Favourite Dream

I started off as a writer
But I wanted to be a fighter
The next day I joined the army
And my best friend there was called Barny

But soon I didn't want to be a fighter anymore
I wanted to walk through the Olympic door
I wanted to be an Olympic swimmer
And I wanted to be an Olympic winner

But once I had won a medal or two
I soon got an awful flu
So now I'm stuck all at home
And sometimes I feel quite alone

The next day I got my final idea
And in my head it was very clear
I could be a singer
And even own a chinchilla

They gave me the job
And I'm in a group with Bob!
They cheered lots at our first gig
And we celebrated with a bowl of figs
Then I woke from my sleep
As my phone went *beep, beep, beep.*

Hikari Daniels (9)
North Hinksey CE Primary School, Oxford

The Battle Of The Dreams

Closing my eyes and entering the world of sleep
I find myself in my second dream that week
Two massive, magnificent mountains, tall and strong
Each topped with a glowing orb, turquoise and ruby
Looking down I find myself sitting on a shadowy spiked dragon
Even further down a battle raged with force on a bloodied field
One as radiant as nature itself
One as dire as death itself
Radiant is led by legion commander, female I presumed
Followed by four of her champions, each with special powers
One on a white horse, dressed in white robes
One slithering about bashing with a mace
One running like the wind shooting with her bow
And one summoning battling trees and teleporting everywhere
On the other side I see a four-legged monster swinging with an axe and teleporting everywhere with his allies
His champion fighters, four again, came with him every time
One on an armoured horse, wreaking havoc with his mace

One reaping souls to make himself more powerful
One slowing her enemies down, making it easier for herself
And one cutting down the trees using his saws
All of it was horrible and I just couldn't look
But suddenly before the end I go through the portal
Again...

Daniel Armstrong (9)
North Hinksey CE Primary School, Oxford

Enter The Dreamland...

Something was padding
Softly behind me
When I turned around, it was gone

A shadowy shape
Sprang out of a rock
It was a jet-black cat

Prowling, it circled me
And softly it hissed
'Come to my paws
Come to my claws
Be careful
Watch your back
And enter the dreamland.'

The moon was covered by clouds
Spreading an eerie darkness upon us
I reached out my hand, and touched the black cat...

It rose to its hind legs
And lifted its paws
The spectacular magic began to happen

Thorn trees rose
They puffed out sparks
The clouds began to clear
'Enter the dreamland,' the cat gently hissed again
'Enter the dreamland, enter the dreamland.'

A world began to slowly appear
Grassy moors and jagged rocks
A crystal clear lake with a swaying boat

I turned around to say thank you
But the cat was gone
Then bit by bit, the world was gone too
The world was just a dream

I looked out of the window
Or was it? I thought
Or was it?

Eva Florence Yoxall-Vale (9)
North Hinksey CE Primary School, Oxford

Dreaming Of 2016

Now let me sleep, don't make a peep,
Where am I going? Where? Where? Where?
I hope it's not a nightmare.

There he is standing tall and great,
David Cameron, it's just too late,
His shoulders drop as he talks of Brexit,
My mind thinks, *I must forget this.*

The carnival music tickles my ears so loud,
Let's party, let's dance, we are in Rio now.
She's standing there with a great big smile,
I think I might be here for a while.
Oh my gosh, I lean in closer,
Bang! Bang! Bang!
She's off, that must be tiring,
Well done, Ellie Simmonds, you're so inspiring.

Now I'm going, my mind's flowing,
Suddenly I hear a cry, where am I and why?
I hear a bomb, it growls at the earth,
There's just no time to lie and wait,
The gravel's crunching beneath my feet,
I run, I run, my heart skips a beat.

This is not a happy ending,
I wish I was at home, in my own bedding.
You might have guessed, I'm at war
This isn't right, people shouldn't have to fight.

Bella Wilson (9)
North Hinksey CE Primary School, Oxford

Lost

I'm upon the grass kneeling low
Where am I? I'll just go with the flow
But now I realise where I am
Why am I here? What's the plan?
Forest, forest, that's all I can see
Miles upon miles it must be
I think, for me, it must be all over
But wait, I've seen a four leaf clover
Hold on, that must mean luck
OK my mind's been struck
Now I can see a bright spark
Shining in the deep, deep dark
It's filling me up with its own brightness
I think I'm starting to be sightless
I'm whirling, I'm twirling all over the place
I can't feel a thing, not even my face
And now I'm back in my bed
No other harm and no more dread.

Verity Broome Saunders (10)
North Hinksey CE Primary School, Oxford

Best Dream

B efore lunch I started a daydream
E verywhere was filled with tropical trees and colourful birds
S urprising shaped clouds danced through the sky
T he trees waved in the air like the grass in the wind

D aydreams can be scary
R ain fell on the beautiful island, bolts of lightning shot all around
E verywhere was drenched in rain, the sea clashed with the sand
A mazingly the sun peeked through the black clouds
M agically the rain disappeared from everywhere and the lightning stopped.

Will Hodges (8)
North Hinksey CE Primary School, Oxford

A Perfect World

Now my mind must drift to sleep
I walk a perfect world
The wars are long gone so I spin and leap
No one's sad or looking glum
There's no more suffering, not a peep
Food's all round and everyone's full
The water is fresh and you let it seep
Now this is a world full of cheer
This is something we should keep
But now I see light and I'm awake
Out of the window I see - the world is a rubbish heap.

Annie Scarborough (10)
North Hinksey CE Primary School, Oxford

The Creeping Cat

Once, when I was asleep at night
I turned into a cat, which gave me a fright
With shimmering fur of a pastel white
And the moon was shining round and bright

Then I saw it, a flash of brown
A little mouse with a tail pointing down
I sharpened my claws
And I lifted my paws

But the mouse was bait
And I was too late
When I thought I was truly dead
I suddenly woke up in bed.

Lucy Desitter (10)
North Hinksey CE Primary School, Oxford

All On A Very Dark Night

The candle danced in the darkness
The books rattled to the music box's tune
The music box's music calmed the lights down
All on a dark night

As I stepped outside
The owls hooted a wonderful tune
Very different from the old music box's
Upset howls came from the wolves in the woods
All on a very dark night.

Nicolas Vargas (7)
North Hinksey CE Primary School, Oxford

My Dream About A Stormy Night

The wind blew hard, the rain pelted down
The soft, comfy rocking chair rocked like a wild horse galloping away
The books shivered on the high up shelves
Windows clattered and the door banged
The tea cups rattled on the hooks
The grass swayed in the horrible weather
And that's when I woke up.

Pippa Scarborough (7)
North Hinksey CE Primary School, Oxford

Untitled

I fell asleep, I was dreaming about a candy land
It was so nice, the sky was as blue as sea
The houses were made from
Chocolate and toffee
The white chocolate sun smiled down
And the sweets tasted lovely

The night before I was dreaming about a haunted house,
I opened the door
There were ghosts, zombies, cobwebs and spiders,
It was so creepy
I opened one door more, I got stuck in cobwebs
The ghosts were there and zombies then I ran away
And then I woke up

Last week I was dreaming about
I was stuck in a never-ending house, I was scared
I opened a door, there was another door and another
I opened about 50 doors then I gave up
Just then I found an axe and knocked down the wall
And I was free

Two weeks ago I was dreaming about
I was a footballer, it was all up to me
If I scored the penalty we'd win the Champions League
I ran up to take the penalty and scored
The crown roared like a lion.

Danny Lewis (9)
St John's Primary School, Edinburgh

My Dream

Late last night
I went to bed as usual
And nothing strange happened
Until...

I dreamed about Candyland
Everything was so sweet
There were giant doughnuts
And a chocolate river

It was all so great until
The dream went black
It slowly came back and
It was horrible monsters
That covered the land and
Spiders

They were all surrounding me
I was petrified, I was shocked
What if they ate me?
Would the dream just end?

Boom!
Where had the monsters gone?
Was I all alone?
I wished they would come back
Even though they were horrid I didn't
Want to be alone

I was crying my heart out
This dream was horrid, I wanted to wake up
I wanted to wake up and be in my bed
Was I stuck in dreamland?

Freya Auchincloss (9)
St John's Primary School, Edinburgh

A Sweet Dream

Dreams are all
Different you see,
They can be anything
You want them to be.
My dream takes place
In a Candy Land,
With a beautiful beach
With sugar instead of sand.

I climb a hard candy rock face,
Looking at more than just the
Human race.
With peppermint pigs and
Chocodiles,
To find these creatures you
Won't have to look for a while.
Chocolate chickens and gummy bears,
These animals are absolutely everywhere.
There are marshmallow mountains
High in the sky,
It's an amazing place, I cannot lie.
The icing grass is the colour of emerald jewels,
No king nor queen
Everyone rules.

Like I said,
Dreams are all
Different you see,
And I think my dream is
The place to be.

Tara Divito (10)
St John's Primary School, Edinburgh

Nightmare

I try to go camping
In the woods
I will get hungry
So I'll take some food

Of course, I didn't know the disaster ahead
But I realised, when a monster took my bread
I suddenly realised I left my camping gear at the car
I was lost and I knew the car was very far
I tried to trace my footsteps from the way I came
And then a bear jumped out at me, hit me with pain
By now, I was running faster than I ever had
I was seeing ugly creatures, was I going mad!
Then I stopped and saw a footprint that was enormous
But when I heard roaring I knew it
Was a dinosaur
I saw it and it came racing like a car
I ran my hardest but it caught up and tore me apart!

Finlay McWilliam (10)
St John's Primary School, Edinburgh

I Closed My Eyes...

I closed my eyes
And fell asleep
And I began to dream...

A cold and frosty winter's day
In the park down by our house.

Whee! Me and my cousins went down the slide
The slide was as fast as a roller coaster ride.

And then we landed on some teddy filling in Santa's workshop.
The fluff was as fluffy as fluffy sheep's wool.

It felt amazing
Santa's beard was as white as the white clouds in the sky.

The machines were huge.
They went *boom, boom, boom.*
As they stamped the buttons on the teddy bears.

Then we went back up the slide
And said, 'That was such an amazing ride.'

Emily McKenzie (10)
St John's Primary School, Edinburgh

My Dream

Last night I went to sleep
Like I always do,
I found myself in Littleroot town.
My powerful Pokémon awoke and stretched
We started another exciting day off
With an adventure in space.

I threw a Masterball,
I shouted, 'Go Rayquaza!'
Roar! went Rayquaza
As we started to soar
Towards a mesmerising meteorite.
We saw the Alpha Pokémon, Arceus,
It was flying gracefully away,
Deoxys following closely behind.
Turning round, Arceus angrily attacks
Deoxys fires a hyper beam.
The two clash together fiercely
Exploding particles fly everywhere
Causing me to awaken from my deep slumber.
I feel exhausted!

James Craig (10)
St John's Primary School, Edinburgh

Once Upon A Dream

The scary woods have
Scary bats and a hut.
Inside the hut there is
A witch brewing potions.
And skeletons in the corner,
Zombies everywhere, slime too.
The water is sludge from the
Giant slugs, the rain is too.

My house is like a witch hut
But much grander than them.
My dog is a little spider and
My cats are vampires
They go out and turns birds into
Little flying zombies.
There are ghosts inside,
They are my friends!

The sky is always black,
The moon is always out.
Cobwebs everywhere.
The place where I get my
Pumpkins is another scary place.
Frankenstein is
Guarding the pumpkins.

Beth Adams (10)
St John's Primary School, Edinburgh

Please Wake Me Up!

There were two boys, me and Phil
Phil is quite peculiar
Our friend Jim invited us to his house
We walked to his house
We went the wrong way.

We saw the mysterious church
We walked in the church
There was a creak from the door
We walked towards the door,
There were cobwebs everywhere
Slam! The door slammed shut.

Then we saw a ghost going by
It came closer and closer
Then we ran as fast as a jaguar
To the nearest door
It was locked
I started to sweat
I could see it coming closer
I felt a tap on my shoulder
'Jim it's time to wake up!'

Nicholas Carr (10)
St John's Primary School, Edinburgh

Sean's Dream

I went to sleep in my bed
And before I knew it
I was at a massive stadium
With excited boys I know,
Taking free kicks
In front of 9 million faces
Scoring the winner
The crowd roaring like a lion.
It was the best goal
Right in top corner
We won 12-2.

I invited them over to my house
To celebrate the victory,
We didn't stay up late
Because we had training the next day
It is meant to be really fun
Since our new manager George Davie
He's the best manager you can ever get
He used to be the best football player
I'm really looking forward to it.

Sean Brannen (9)
St John's Primary School, Edinburgh

Bright Future

I am travelling to Oxford
My family are with me.
I feel happy as a bee.
But I am as nervous as a shy person.
But why am I travelling?
Because I am going to study at Oxford University.
I get out of the car, say bye to my family.
Now, I feel sad as a lonely ant.
The rain jumped down making dripping sounds.
I ran in the building as fast as a cheetah.
When I went in I said to myself...
Let's be as strong as a lion.
And after 4 years I became a
Cardiologist.
And I was as smart as an owl.

Motiya Muzzamil (9)
St John's Primary School, Edinburgh

Untitled

I fly to Neptune
In a Formula One supercar

Then I see a half scorpion
Half tarantula

And Neptune is
As cold as Antarctica

The half scorpion
Half tarantula
Is as big as Africa

I land on Neptune
With a thump,
I defeat the half scorpion
Half tarantula

Neptune is made out
Of chocolate and
Mint, and the stars
Are as big as an
Elephant

I am the saviour of the world
All the flying pigs thank me
And they make me their pig god.

Himmat Singh (10)
St John's Primary School, Edinburgh

Untitled

In Dreamland
I'm amazing at football,
I'm as fast as a cheetah,
The pitch is like sweet home.

My best friend is Paul Pogba
He gives me loads of confidence.
We like playing together.
Everyone wants our autograph.

On the pitch, I'm
As cool as a carrot,
As cunning as a fox,
As skilful as an Olympian.

My house has
A lovely candy spiral,
A hard fudge door,
A sprinkling chimney,
And candyfloss windows.

When I wake up
I feel different.

Grant Daly (10)
St John's Primary School, Edinburgh

Death's Gift

Today is going to be the best
dream ever I bet you
So in the dream

I created a potion
That makes all dead rise.

Then after I made it
I was very proud.

So I used it, all dead rose
But not as I thought
They were zombies and as you guess
Everybody was running for their lives
But they'd soon be zombies as well.

But I stayed and thought if
I created them they must listen to me
And then I realised I'm Cyprian.

Cyprian Kreft (10)
St John's Primary School, Edinburgh

Dreamland

Last night I went to sleep
And I woke up to realise I was not in my room
I looked around and saw a VR and some
Game posters
Then I knew I was in Gamingland.

Where eating a mushroom makes you grow
You can jump on clouds like a monkey
Gaming is the only work you do
Consoles and other gaming platforms are free
You don't pay taxes and membership
Black and green are popular colours
I suddenly woke up to remember...
It was a dream.

Imran Zafar (9)
St John's Primary School, Edinburgh

Creepy Land

Zombie eating flesh
Ghosts flying high in the sky
Vampires looking for blood
Wolves howling
Skeletons lying everywhere
Headless horses running about

Poisonous fountain
Deadly spiders
Scary monsters
Bats hanging upside down
Zombies walking all over the town
Hunting for rotten flesh

And then I woke up, it was only a dream.

George Davie (10)
St John's Primary School, Edinburgh

My Dream

I fell asleep one night
I had an extraordinary dream
I was surrounded by unicorns
And rainbows

I was with all my friends
I was frightened yet excited
Rainbows were dancing up high
Unicorns were prancing

I woke up, I was confused
Was it a dream or was it true?
I was amazed what dreams
Can do.

Callie Dooner (10)
St John's Primary School, Edinburgh

Ghost Town

In my dream I woke up
But there was no one else around
It was pitch-black outside
No lights to be seen.

I saw a creature outside
With the moonlight glowing on it
I saw it moving closer
What was it?

Alex Roy (10)
St John's Primary School, Edinburgh

Creepy Land

It is a creepy place
Spiderwebs on trees with blood on them
Headless horses running wildly
Giant poisonous spiders on skeletons
Poison fountains
Crawling zombies with blood coming
Out of their eyes.

Lewis Johnston
St John's Primary School, Edinburgh

Not Everything That It Seems

I entered the school at 9.30am
I shouted, 'Sorry I'm late,' but nobody was there
All the shelves had nothing on
There was nothing inside except an old, wooden book
I opened it
I heard a stamp on the floor
I turned
It was a teacher, not my teacher, nobody's teacher, even in the school
Was she a ghost?
She cannot be
I tried talking to her but no response
I grabbed the teacher by the arm
It was my moment to...
See if she was a ghost
She flew away through the walls and she was never seen again
I walked home and thought about the adventure that I'd just had
It was just a dream...

Jodie Marie Leigh (10)
Thornley Primary School, Durham

The Magical Forest

One day I saw them there,
In this magical forest.
All of a sudden fairy dust fell on me,
I did not know what was happening.
I saw something flying over there,
What could it be?
Wow, it was small fairies!
They were joined by a unicorn,
Which was rather pretty.
It had a long, pointy, sparkly horn,
And long, colourful hair,
I stopped and stared for a while,
But then it was time to go.
Home was only a few miles away,
So I said my goodbyes and went.

Katie Elves (10)
Thornley Primary School, Durham

There Was A Bowl

There was a bowl
A wooden bowl
A wooden, colourful bowl
And in that bowl
There was a peach
A juicy peach
A small, juicy peach
And in this peach
There was a pip
A round pip
A round, brown pip
And in this pip
There was a dream
A beautiful dream
A beautiful, wild dream
And in this dream
There was a sparkle
A bright sparkle
A bright, diamond sparkle
And in this sparkle
Was hope.

Lilia Grace Mains (10)
Thornley Primary School, Durham

Once Upon A Dream

Lying in my bed,
Slowly drifting away,
I walk upon the clouds,
Inside my head.

I walk for miles and miles,
Until I see,
An unknown world,
Presented in front of me.

I venture into the world of unknown,
Still in a dream,
In there I find,
An angel flying away.

Still in my land of pure love,
I feel something beginning to happen,
My world fades away,
I am awake.

Millie Nuttall (10)
Thornley Primary School, Durham

The Dark Cave

There was a dream
A scary dream
A scary, mysterious dream
And in this dream
Was a cave
A dark cave
A cold, dark cave
And in this cave
Was a dragon
A humongous dragon
A humongous, red dragon
And on this dragon
There were fangs
Bloody fangs
Bloody, sharp fangs
What have I done?
Will I survive?
I start to shake...

Ben Hall (10)
Thornley Primary School, Durham

Dreams Come True

Upon my dream
I wish I was a gymnast
Like Amy Tinkler
Doing gymnastics through a sprinkler
I wish I had skills
Going up hills

Upon my dream
I wish I was a dancer
Like the reindeer Prancer
Training in a beautiful ball
In the awesome fall.

Emma Jane Stokoe (10)
Thornley Primary School, Durham

Spiders!

S piders are creepy
P ossibly the scariest thing ever
I hate them with a passion!
D own the wall they climb
E specially in autumn
R unning and jumping as fast as can be
S piders are not welcome in my family.

Benjamin Jack Hardy (10)
Thornley Primary School, Durham

Once Upon A Dream

My dream is to be a Pokémon
In an amazing Pokéball
I explore the land on a quest
I gotta catch 'em all

Which Pokémon is wise?
Which Pokémon shall I be?
A Pikachu would be nice
Or even a Legendary

Which... ohhh a Mr Mime
I would have a creepy face
My hair would be dark as night
Darker than deepest space

Shall I be a Charizard
A dragon with giant wings
I would be as big as a tree
I'll wake up when Jigglypuff sings

Say I'm a Raichu
An evolved yellow beast
I'll beat the gym with all my might
While eating a delicious feast

I can see Brock
Getting ready to battle me
He sends out his Onyx
I'll win this battle you'll see.

Sam Halliday (11)
Thornton Dale CE Primary School, Pickering

Once Upon A Dream

Paris 2024
Olympic crowd goes wild
I am unstoppable
The stadium shines in my eyes
I stand on the green pitch
The clock ticking in my ears
Then the silver whistle chimed
My nerves started taking over
I knew I couldn't let anyone down
The sweat dripped from my head
Drip, drip, drip, drip
I ran to the ball
As fast as a leopard
Then my confidence ate my nerves
The half-time whistle, it was a tie
Then after half-time
Whoosh!
The ball hit the back of the net
We were winning
The final whistle blew
We had won Paris 2024 Olympics.

Kara Peel (10)
Thornton Dale CE Primary School, Pickering

Once Upon A Dream

The arena of jumps are set
Can we do it? My heart's pounding
The chairs are full of billions of people
My family are cheering me on over the scary jumps
When I get through to the next round
My family are going wild in the crowd
Me and my horse are tired and sweaty
Drip, drip, drop
Next day the final round
Of show jumping, can we do it?
A sudden boost of confidence
Comes to my head
We are in, can we do it?
We're against the clock
We get over the scary jumps
We did it!
My family are so loud
I am so proud
The moment of truths came true.

Anna Todd (9)
Thornton Dale CE Primary School, Pickering

Once Upon A Dream

Tokyo 2020
Olympic crowd goes wild
Every step closer
More nerves kick in
GB tracksuit off
Goggles on
The moment of truth
The crowd falls silent
My heart races like a cheetah
I step on the starting block
Boom
I start my race with excitement
Springing off the starting block
Gliding through the glistening water
I do a terrific tumble turn
I get in the lead
Only 50 metres to go
Can I do this?
Do I believe in myself?
I touch the end
I look at the screen
And I won!

Evie Atkinson (10)
Thornton Dale CE Primary School, Pickering

Once Upon A Dream

I dream of having the most wonderful house
With two kids and a pug
My kids upon my roller coaster
And my pug is trying to chase after them
I can see the Hollywood sign
But my pug is gone
So I go inside
And my living room is a dump
And then there is my pug
Eating a box of twenty chicken nuggets
Then in the background there is a bang
And my microwave is gone
But then my kid starts to cry
Because his chocolate bar is gone
But now it's the end of the day
And things are still going *bang!*

Nathan Bowes (9)
Thornton Dale CE Primary School, Pickering

Once Upon A Dream

I felt shocked with excitement
My heart was beating fast
I was giggling for ages
Is this real?
I saw all the lovely lights
My hair was blowing like waves
The moment has come
I was muttering to myself,
'This is, this is the best day ever'
My friends were giggling
My hair was smooth as silk
I saw the fluffy sheep land
The hotel was waiting for me
My tummy waiting for a hot chocolate
My heart was racing
Then I started to head back
My hot chocolate was racing.

Ruby Lunn (10)
Thornton Dale CE Primary School, Pickering

Once Upon A Dream

The machine whirs to life
A doorway appears
I wonder with my ears
Where will it take me today
Perhaps a lab in Pompeii
Full of experiments fizzing and whizzing
Or maybe a windsurf competition
My teacher is winning
The crowds are cheering
The wind is blowing
And Miss is saving the day
But I must be asleep
For Miss can't windsurf
And labs don't exist in Pompeii
So I must be dreaming
As deep as a bottomless pit...

Andrew Prole (10)
Thornton Dale CE Primary School, Pickering

Once Upon A Dream

My coach was smiling,
Everyone started cheering for me.
I couldn't let them down.
The bars were waiting,
Could I do it?
The chalk was on my hands,
Sweat was dripping
Drip, drip, drip!
The fear was taking over.
The big beam,
My family were watching over.
Everything was ready,
It was time.
Suddenly I slipped,
My heart was racing.
I could feel confidence,
The strength was in me,
I could win...

Molly Gwilliam (10)
Thornton Dale CE Primary School, Pickering

Once Upon A Dream

I dive into the pool
The water splashing
The crowds cheering
Now is my time to shine

My heart pounding
I swim until I'm a torpedo
Getting ahead of everyone

I keep smiling
And as I'm on my second lap
Someone overtakes me
I swim to my heart's content
And suddenly I cross the line and...
I have won!

Adam Halliday (9)
Thornton Dale CE Primary School, Pickering

Once Upon A Dream

This is the moment
Can I do it?
Me and my colleagues set off
I feel nervous but excited
We slowly walked over
My heart was thumping
This is it
We need to save the poorly puppy
I saw the injection
The needle
Pop!
I had done it
I felt proud
Inside, my heart felt amazing.

Libby Horsley (10)
Thornton Dale CE Primary School, Pickering

Once Upon A Dream

My elephant was ready
Walking through the forest
The wet grass
The elephant's trunk
I feel excited
I feel amazed
My hair flowing
The wind is cool
My elephant is big
Crunch
The leaves on the floor
Crunching
Down the path
In the forest
Is it real
Or a dream...?

Leah Rouph (10)
Thornton Dale CE Primary School, Pickering

Once Upon A Dream

The computer works
The Internet connects
I click record
I record my 'Let's play'
My subs go up
My dream is coming true
Just as I finished...
My computer crashed
Could this be the end?
Inside I felt like a failure
But I wasn't too upset
I posted the video in time!

Hollie Buckler (10)
Thornton Dale CE Primary School, Pickering

Once Upon A Dream

I start the engine
Going up and up
I can't believe it
I'm driving a plane!
I land near the velodrome
I jump on my bike
Zoom round the arena
A glistening gold medal
A world record!
A party
Just for me
Lots of famous people
My whole family
I'm so proud.

Emma Hall (10)
Thornton Dale CE Primary School, Pickering

Once Upon A Dream!

Strutting down the red carpet
I feel good!
Signing autographs and posing for photos
Fans are screaming, screaming for me!
I'm admired by millions
Flashing lights, photographers
We walk into the cinema
Take our seats
The room goes dark
The movie begins...

Sarah Vasey (10)
Thornton Dale CE Primary School, Pickering

Once Upon A Dream

I dream of being a famous knitter
My needles are driving me mad
I am trying to follow the pattern
The crowds are cheering
My needles are cold
I can feel the warm sand
My family are going mad
What if I don't win?
What am I going to do?

Katie Jeal (9)
Thornton Dale CE Primary School, Pickering

Once Upon A Dream

My dream is to be a millionaire
My servants respect me
I have lots of marvellous money
I get into my lovely limousine
My fortress has a pass code
I own a crunching crocodile
I am proud
Of my glorious home
My crocodile eats juicy meat.

Charles Edward Coultas (9)
Thornton Dale CE Primary School, Pickering

Once Upon A Dream

I am king
Now I feel awesome
America, England are mine
I am happier than a dog
When it sees a bone
Emeralds and rubies
Are awesome
I have wind blowing
And my brighter than a star armour
There's no turning back now.

Kai Smith (10)
Thornton Dale CE Primary School, Pickering

Once Upon A Dream

My bike is ready
Jumping over rocks
My friends near me
Fearing crashes
Skidding
Falling off
My bike breaking
Feeling like I won
Being the best
I'm scared it might break
It broke
Quick fix time.

Harry Gibbon (10)
Thornton Dale CE Primary School, Pickering

Once Upon A Dream

The curtains were opening
People getting into positions
The music starts to come on
I'm ready
We had all started our routine
The clicking of cameras rang through my ears
Was I going to become a student in the academy?

Tasha Musgrave (10)
Thornton Dale CE Primary School, Pickering

Once Upon A Dream

Slippy mud
I am shaking
Sweat trickled
The track is ready
The bike is ready
And so was I!
3, 2, 1, we were off
Can I make it?
Can I do it?
Do I have what it takes?

Ashley Smith (10)
Thornton Dale CE Primary School, Pickering

Once Upon A Dream

I dream of being
The best in the tent
Winning the judges
Mary Berry and Paul Hollywood
So scary
I can see cakes
Food, table and ingredients
I'm so excited to
Win!

Lily-Mae Gascoyne (10)
Thornton Dale CE Primary School, Pickering

Once Upon A Dream

My workshop
In India
The hazy sky
Looking at me
It's time to test
Will it work?
I'm off to the fire
I never thought
Chocolate was
So heavy!

Ellen Hudson (9)
Thornton Dale CE Primary School, Pickering

Once Upon A Dream

There it was, the best ship
I was in it
It was really big
The countdown began
Five, four, three, two, one...
Blast off!
Whoosh!

Lewis Wade (9)
Thornton Dale CE Primary School, Pickering

Young Writers
Est.1991

YOUNG WRITERS INFORMATION

We hope you have enjoyed reading this book – and that you will continue to in the coming years.

If you're a young writer who enjoys reading and creative writing, or the parent of an enthusiastic poet or story writer, do visit our website **www.youngwriters.co.uk**. Here you will find free competitions, workshops and games, as well as recommended reads, a poetry glossary and our blog.

If you would like to order further copies of this book, or any of our other titles, then please give us a call or visit **www.youngwriters.co.uk**.

Young Writers
Remus House
Coltsfoot Drive
Peterborough
PE2 9BF
(01733) 890066
info@youngwriters.co.uk